Toddler Yoga
In the Park

Written by Theresa Del Vecchio

For more information visit her website:
qtkidsbooks.com

THIS BOOK BELONGS TO

_____

IT'S TIME TO STRETCH
AND RELAX A BIT.
ROLL YOUR YOGA MAT OUT AND
GET READY TO SIT.

SIT UP TALL AND TAKE A DEEP BREATH IN FROM YOUR nose,
COUNT TO THREE AND BLOW OUT FROM YOUR MOUTH UNTIL THE AIR REACHES YOUR TOES!

DO IT AGAIN A FEW TIMES THROUGH, AS YOU NOTICE ALL OF THE BEAUTIFUL NATURE AROUND YOU.

THE SOFT BREEZE BLOWING IN
YOUR HAIR,
AND THE SOUND OF THE BIRDS
CHIRPING IN THE AIR.

NOW WE ARE IN THE RIGHT MINDSET TO START.
GET READY, BECAUSE THIS IS THE BEST PART!

TREE POSE

BALANCE ONE FOOT ON THE GROUND AS YOU BRING YOUR ARMS UP HIGH, THEN GENTLY TOUCH THE BOTTOM OF YOUR FOOT TO THE INSIDE OF YOUR THIGH.

DUCK POSE

TURN YOUR FEET OUT
AND BEND YOUR KNEES,
YOU CAN COME DOWN
AS LOW AS YOU PLEASE.

WARRIOR 2 POSE

STAND NICE AND STRONG
WITH YOUR LEGS WIDE APART,
TURN ONE FOOT OUT AND BEND
WHILE YOU REACH YOUR ARMS
AWAY FROM YOUR HEART!

DOWNWARD DOG POSE

START WITH YOUR HANDS AND FEET ON THE FLOOR, NEXT PULL YOUR HIPS UP TO THE SKY UNTIL THEY CAN'T GO UP ANYMORE!

COBRA POSE

LAY ON YOUR BELLY WITH YOUR FEET ON THE FLOOR, NOW REACH YOUR ARMS FORWARD AND PICK UP YOUR CHEST SOME MORE!

CAT COW POSE

GENTLY COME DOWN TO THE GROUND ON YOUR HANDS AND FEET WITH EASE. BREATHE IN AND LOOK UP, THEN SCOOP YOUR BELLY UP AND LOOK DOWN AS YOU BREATHE OUT TO RELEASE.

TRIANGLE POSE

BOTH FEET ARE ON THE MAT AND ONE FOOT IS TURNED OUT, REACH DOWN TO THE TURNED FOOT AND REACH THE OTHER ARM ABOUT.

THAT WAS FUN!

WHICH YOGA POSE IS YOUR FAVORITE ONE?

About the Author

Other books by Theresa Del Vecchio

Cotton Candy Skies and French Fries
Apple Pies and Hayrides
Cocoa Calling and Snowflakes Falling
Ice Cream Treats and Baseball Cleats
Ella's Wonderfully Wild Hair
Chippy the Grateful Squirrel: The Tale
of the Tasty Pumpkin
A Trip to Turtle Back Zoo
All About Sea Turtles
Pancakes with Pop Pop
What Do Nanas Do?
Beach Baby Yoga

Theresa Del Vecchio's passion for writing blossomed during her elementary school days. This love for storytelling deepened even more as she embraced the roles of a teacher and a parent. Through her experiences, she has published several books, celebrating the joys we find in our everyday lives. Writing is not just a hobby for her; it's a way to share the beauty of life's simple moments!

www.ingramcontent.com/pod-product-compliance
Lightning Source LLC
Chambersburg PA
CBHW041553040426
42447CB00002B/174